Stardust

Anthony Ray Pipkin

Copyright © 2024 by Anthony Ray Pipkin

First paperback edition 2024

Anuci Press edition 2024

www.anuci-press.com

Cover Design by DaliaVerse Designs (photo by Jeremy Thomas on Unsplash)

ISBN 979-8-9914345-3-9 (paperback)

ISBN 979-8-9914345-4-6(eBook)

Contents

Foreward

It was 1997 in Deep Ellum, Texas. I was in my favorite haunt, when I noticed Anthony. He seemed a bit dislocated, but I could tell he was drinking up the essence of the room. I asked him if he was there to see the band. He told me he had just come from the Java Lounge and their open mic poetry reading. He said he was a writer. Being a lover of the written word and a fan of Jim Carrol, I was eager to read his poetry. From there, we created a beautiful friendship over cocktails, words, and the Book of Nods.

In the cloistered seclusion of a cabin in Honey Grove, Texas to long walks in Tennyson Park, Anthony reached out and drew words from his introspective observation of society. As he reels from numbing cocktails, the nakedness of his childlike soul is revealed. His artistic energy is at once laconic and vibrating. His words are punctuated by the undeniable wisdom of an old soul, with the uncanny clarity in a realm where pithy is an art of the first degree. Anthony's mind never stops writing as this is a reference of his life. His guile is hidden in his beauty, while behind the recesses of his enigmatic mind are thoughts impossible to guess. Anthony has created a divine spark with words that describe the emblematic moments of his life as his teenage years escape, and he evolves into a poet.

These are free verses about those who matter. A frank, haunting examination of one poet's personal and spiritual quest and a lifelong journey of discovery. Anthony's influences of Jim Carroll, Walt Whitman, Bob Dylan, and Hunter S. Thompson shine through, making this cluster of poems a cathartic literary endeavor.

Terri Jackson

Dedication

For my mother,
Karen T. Pipkin

-Sunshine ridden vacant shores,
purple lavishly laden skies.
Rusty ravished streets;
stardust flying by.-

Birds on the Wire

Now I cater to the starving souls shaking galleries
from their heads. Passionate winds cry blind in
the sky. Soon the twenty year rain will wash our
trail of tears away. Stand clear, the clouds are ancient
pride.

Who waits there? Under dreaded locks of golden hair,
such crystal blue eyes under fortunate skies. Follow
me, I have conquered the walls that have long been
our boundaries. We can move mountains amid stormy
weather, forever cradle fallen stars together. Do
you feel pain? How does it strike? Like thunder
in the errant gray sky. Follow me forever, you and
I chasing the wind together, Learning to fly.

Indian Wizard

Great solitude was shuddered upon the new waking
day, more dusty visions since cluttered, and borrowed
a reference to fray.

The lull of a new sun is now pitted and hurriedly
grazes the land, once followed here the Indian Wizard,
hath time dealt him a rotten hand. Under the pale
blue moon seated, the proudest of that sacred
clan. Watching as father time uplifted and washed
their truths within the sand.

Tears no longer flirt nor flow upon this riverous
land, where the Indian Wizard is still living, and
playing the devil's hand.

Capricorn Gold

To this world I wish to speak, my hair has grown
leaves, now shedding temples before me. Time riddled
gallows have sold their fortunes, slowly marching,
treading between the haze of a new sunny day.

The elder of ancient remedies, the most profound
tyranny, a soul guarded by none. Praise the day
stretched out before us, father time shall darken
the sun.

No darkness ever seeded so deep, silent sprits slowly
creeping, boarding the windows, pacing, waiting,
chains dangling in between the midnight offering.

Dear fate has left a bitter torch. No clarity of
sight, only the still of the night delivering silent

oaths. Days times three culminate the breeze, one
upon another, spacing out the rusty dim lit memories.

Most gallant deliverance, cherish the rip tides that
bleed. Caress this rolling ocean, forgoing shattered
notions, remember the faith that I breed.

An existence ill-fated, binding the clouds, changing
to black. My prayers live in these words, assuring
the truth eventually shall stack.

In Love Only Shall We Trust

Pleased to meet such a fair lady so sweet, precious
and daring the eyes which we meet.

Pardon my behavior, it is true I sometimes stare,
still I am curious and wonder if I were to caress
your hair, might I find the softest of daisies holding
peace and prayer.

Shall we take a walk, your hand upon mine, through
more wondrous hills and rivers most divine?

Leaving our rivals here to rust; heading towards
the sun, in love only shall we trust.

Waste

Fallen stars sliver silver down shaky walls, with
bells of gold that echo the halls. The clambering
and staggering, the timeless reminder, the lost memory.
A somber pace, a cautious face, dear saddened scenery.

These slow aging ways with their poisoned seeds,
they cast about our fate; counting souls and taking
toll for everything we hate.

The Last Millenium

Splendid scenery covering me, shading my face, an
aurora of colors all around, sparkling light shivering
my own eyes lingering can see, yet to these deaf
ears, no precious sounds.

Birds in their graceful motion fly thinly through
the air, sparing my innocence, making no sound of
their own no violent flare, giving only sparkling
visions aloft this scenery we share.

From me to you, these moments are few, I beg you
for your time. The last three moons have held a
different hue, breaking the path I fly, spreading
the stars vainly through the air, lighting up the
heavenly sky.

Night Watch

The cold, damp, lime green evening grass, three raving
dogs between the starlight pass, the small one sort
of orange, the skinny one glowing white, the larger
was a thundering black.

With a vicious intensity, their blood red curious
nighttime eyes fed relentlessly on the luminous,
yellowish lamplight flickering spontaneously, flirting
with the music in the air.

And there alone I stare, relaxing in my evening chair,
do not dare distract three dogs in a pack, might
they charge and attack, drag me away, bury my blood
damp bones by the garbage out back.

Trees

Trees: abundant with limbs, branches, voluminous
clusters of leaves appearing to me as thousands of
eyes folding outward and in, covering the full circle
of life, creeping in on each day, present and past,
closing in on the future.

Trees: immortal, everlasting, luring the stars,
bracing the heavens, holding with pride, ancient
yet modern. Counting the years of grief, the years
of joy, eternal homage, eternal stardom.

Trees: shouldering the air, swaying, breathing,
most honorable mission. Carry on, gallant, destined
fortress of nature, guiding the children of misfortune
through the churning years, perpetual shelter of
flowing tears.

Side Show

What's the camera show? Open windowpane, foggy
mist on a mid-summer day, I really couldn't say,
how the story goes, how it rolls and plays and shades
my face from the pain that eats away day after day
after passing the blade from here to there to God
knows where and back again to a time where the wind
blows free and sane people who play the games they
play and free their mind of horrible things.

Still the torch we see burns free, burns clean, then
turns green with passion and greed that leads the
passing people through garden streets, guarded kings
and promised queens, through the pale blue sea, crystal
clear reflection of you and me, others fall to the
side and bleed with fire, burn with rain; as we
try to make sense of the darker side of things.

Time Dance

Take my hand dear child, follow me down this tarnished
road. Given a chance we'll shine like stars forever
blown.

Here we'll build our home upon this spacious land,
engrave our names, forget the shame, bury our treasures
beneath the sand.

To pass the candle through the breeze, our star blown
souls forever free. We change our ways to erase
the days of misery, the days of tyranny.

These voices keep their solemn pace, this path we've
chose to lead us straight. Singing songs of fallen
thrones, counting out the days, the dance of time unfolds.

Transcendent

The story was told to me, constantly reminding me,
weird visions, singing sermons, sweetly, softly, scenery
lapsing into fever red.

She approached me faintly, caressed my blushing cheeks
with the familiar touch I remember so well, as if
it were yesterday, free as the wind in May, a child
who knows of no such boundaries, flying with ease
the breeze of the day.

As she pointed her finger to the west there soon appeared
towering mountains never before seen by eyes so green,
deep tainted valleys with powerful waterfalls to replenish
the hazy mountain side.

In the distance comes the sound of the southbound

train passing frantically, pushing, treading, seeking
the homage of their virgin homeland. A timid breeze
runs swiftly through strands of curly blonde hair,
then kisses my dry lips with the sweet touch of mist.

At the end of the day, the steam from those trains
now blown far away, the scent of her hair no longer
here for me to breathe. I pass lonely with the music
of the streets, as the sunrise wakes early in the
east, deaf and numb I wonder through time and lost
dreams, silent, transcendent.

Soul Tides

Out with my comrades, toiling the evening tide; at
the last hours of dusk we scale the jagged mountain
side.

Hiking the winding trail with uncommon vigor, choosing
to be alone amongst ourselves. God's abandoned children,
stranded singers; of fortune, fame, ancient battles,
swirling prey, of lifetimes passing lonely, all so
different, yet all the same.

Counting stars so far away, our shining souls forever
roaming. Dragging dreams along the way, losing track
of where were going.

The Trail We Tread

My breath is yours, as your breath is mine. I cry
with you as you so many times have cried with me.

On the eve of disaster, I pray you will never desert
me, never leave me so cold and broken down. I'll summon
abandoned stars to slither faithfully down, shape
a circlet of loving light upon your brow.

Though the path we cover is no longer new, may seem
tangled, a harsh, bitter journey, cluttered with hills
jagged and stoned.

My hand with your hand, each heart beating as one.

Ocean

The tide rolls through in crystalline blue, blowing
a spiritual breeze. Henceforth, never will this day
be forgotten.

Great birds of grand oceans climb high, and they fly
with uncommon valor. Such beauty never have I seen
before this day, only read of through wise men's scrolls.

A fortunate soul sets sail and flows through channels
of mystical potions. Beauty is freedom; freedom
is the ocean.

Sun Day

Today I write splendid dreams, beautiful horizons,
fallible scenes, shimmering fluorescent mountains
pouring green. A picture in my mind spread out in
front of me.

The Sunrise red, bright in my head, clings close to
me and brings rival dreams not yet been fed. My senses
are real, caressing rapid delirious shrills, fevering
the tides that I feel, treading on towards the path
I have killed.

Imagery

The meadows sprinkled haze with dusk, early morning sunlight, yellow burning rays from downward the shallow blue sky they thrust.

The mist on the grass, on my feet, flawless sparrow flying above, curiously sensing her noble surroundings, catching the wind beneath.

The wind blowing vehement potions through the air around me, spinning off celestial colors for me to see. Painted a picture of this glorious scene, these loyal surroundings, to see again from some rainy day, to swim into and fade away, my soul to drown in and fly away.

A Song for the Spring

A passing angel surely sent this heavenly day just
for me to revel in. The lustrous clouds shimmering,
outlying blue, thick white glimmering, pillowy wind
running through.

Sunlight lowly lingering between leafless limbs of
abundant trees. The fresh breath of spring blows
freely, for me, for you, if you shall forever believe
its truth.

For nature, in its mystic ways, the only true shades
I see, constantly following me. For the musing birds
gliding superbly from tree to tree. Singing melodies
pure and sweet as I caress my winter scarred cheeks,
this song is for thee.

Yet on this day that teases spring, I know only
one love could surely bring for me, those countless
passions my tattered heart sings.

Lights Out

Passion breeds excess freedom. Freedom of mind, heart
and soul. It cannot be taught, nor can it be learned.
Only can it be seeded inside you at the first moment,
the first breath, then passed on to the next believer
on your death bed.

In the end, when the once bright flames of passion
dull to a lowly flicker of hope, who will pass their
freedom to the next, when it's all dead and gone.

These Days Neverending

What if the days should cease to pass? When would
the nighttime come, when shall the evening cast it's
ghastly frown.

Will ever the full moon glow again where shimmering
stars make their home? Lost in outer channels, enveloped
around the sun, rotating within the clouds, captured
between the midday rain.

Sprout, surge forth proud darkness forgotten; shall
the burning rays of daylight ever pass; my heart
yearns for sullen black, sing your haunting song to
me at last.

I, like the phantom owl, loathe the day, cannot bear
its sweltering ways. Prosperous is the light, I see
well in its surroundings. Yet my energy loses life,
forgets the imminent boundaries.

In my bed I lie still, hence the midnight hour rolls
freely, I feel the swirling wind of wisdom; it speaks
soft; what rolling emotions this lonely heart springs,
when at night the eyes are blind though the ears are
keen.

The Dancer

The ballerina delicately swaying to and fro, silent
steps, spacing, falling one upon the next.

Exact, pure, sweet dance of nature. Casting eyes
to the air, not to stare into my lonely eyes.

Her beauty bound by silence. Left only to dance the
sweet words of love across an empty stage into my
fair blue sea.

Save my tender soul, give you lucid dance for my empty
arms to forever hold.

Night Owl

The starlight path funnels through, stretching out the
evening sky. Daytime crumbles slowly to the ground
watching with heedful eyes.

Gray birds of the night, hid within lofty trees;
soon they shall disembark, begin their flight, lift
their wings to catch the swirling breeze.

Whilst snowy winters capture distant lands where darkness
settles strongly, here I lay in southern hands amid
the midday heat, awaiting the midnight calling.

Streets

These streets live intensely, immensely, and always curiously inside a vivid imagination.

Quietly pondering, reflecting, peacefully leaving me, or me leaving them, vacant and empty; hollow streets that live alone.

Recession

I shall not laugh at the cries of others, their heart and
soul beckons me.

I shall never possess things which do not become me,
for I am only unique in my own eyes.

I shall never search for people and places which are
meant to be lost, for they have lives of their own,
and wish not to be found.

I shall never dwell again on the past, lost far beyond
my reach, those days have wings, they care less of
memories, make no familiar sounds.

A Midnight Daze

Awoke from yet another scanty dream. A meager understanding,
sparsely decorated black and white scene.

Ever perpetual land, bold yet trivial, comical and
tranquil, sarcastic but sensual, sauntering stardust
sand.

Entering cleverly somewhat nimbly, still nobly receiving
the clever black and white haze. I walked backwards
for a while to see my footprints erased.

Impalpable being might I be, no one other besides
me have I seen; I do believe I am luminous with bright
eyes to see.

I shadow boxed for a moment with a black and white

shadow reflecting more capricious than I. The shade
was obscure and hidden.

A neglected garden smiled, tarnished by the absence
of rain, still the fragrant flowers of spring gave
real life for me to breathe.

The foiled and frowned daughters passing through gates,
watching their father's toil with hate; and the prisoners
go further down the scythe of time to meet the dogs
of hell who wait to suffocate the mime.

A Cry for the Blind, A Cry for the Lonely

Whoever so much as cradles reason and doubt between
the same two arms, threatens themselves with endless
compromise.

As we yearn for laughter, we also yearn to cry, our
lives flow like riverous potions, constantly heeding
nature's grind, searching evermore man's eventual ocean;
hoping for Venus wings to secure our flight.

Though we wish for wings to fly skyward, never to
come down, living happily in the air, when shall we
pray for aquatic lungs to fill our breast, so we may
then swim the sea onward towards the celestial years,
singing songs of hopes and fears, following the path

of fallen peers.

The Autumn Wake

Queen of the midnight sea, an angel of time ridden
dreams, surging through channels misty, unknown.
Passing fierce the curiously winding stream.

Here's to you, so sweet, the purest, the fairest
most equitable season. A toast from me to you, cherish
this day, lock away for keeps, my life is yours for the
taking.

Autumn closes in without fear, receiving my noble
offering. Ripe ole season, so brisk, so cool, abundantly
free, simmering starlight sauntering.

The summer I fever no more, her patterns have parted.
Peeking through my morning door, the autumn wake has
started.

Killing Creed

Shadowed fortresses upon these dim gray walls; suggestive
obscurity, holy wars, ancient battles, the rise to profound
power, the tragic death, ultimate downfall.

Swaying oak trees standing definite, innocent, silent
life; still breathing swiftly, yielding a sweet breeze
cautiously towards me. I breath with them and because
of them.

They stand everlasting the vacant, rusty, hallow bodied
streets. Withstood the test of time, wars of years
long passed, weathered the cold frost of winters
untimely sleet. Survived the thirsty years of summers
lasting heat.

So fond in the belief that men's wrong doings, our

senseless wars, starving greed, drowning grief; someday
shall cease and rise to revel in nature's reefs, protect
her boundaries, take the oath of sanity, converge
and halt the damnation, the killing creed.

Southern Homage

Preposterous is the heat on this day, no careless
southern wind, no sympathy to heal these tattered
wings.

Visions of beautiful landscapes take hold of my sight,
capture my soul; the ruby red sun caresses the sky,
dusty with gold.

Those pure southerly men, destined boys of summer,
shining forever under gallant eyes, beneath the velvet
rays. Dancing triumphantly, holding with grace, running
down memories cluttered with days.

The Noose

Days since passed have gained my recognition, to
roam about and play between the rhymes of yesterday,
to dance and chance the game of unknown reason.

I persuade myself at times; (times I remember well),
to believe in sacred things. So often we drown and
suffer, we dwell on vibrant moonlit nights, hence
we blame our common themes.

The muse who releases tension, the rope so tightly
wrapped, the noose of apprehension.

Drift Weed

I shattered a beer bottle in the street, almost hurt
an innocent child. I felt a tad bit tired, sort of
sad, kind of weak, wiped away the days last smile.

I chose a path near this alley, walked curiously between
these weeds arching over the fences full of graffiti,
all this time Zeppelin tunes ran through my head.
This lady ragged and wretched asked for some spare
change, said her kids needed fed. I sensed she was
lying but took her words for truth's sake, for the
children's sake, if there really were any.

I continued, stumbling, rumbling, falling in front
of my feet, standing myself back up, wandering in
circles, round and round, waiting for someone to knock
me back down, to crack my teeth beneath against the

concrete.

Another song danced through my head; it was I believe
Dylan instead. Subterranean Homesick Blues, I remember
now, it leaked from my ears, found my lips, fed me
the words, I sang slowly, keeping rhythm with my feet,
still frequently tripping and falling down, the sound
of the ground catching my face, scattering words from
my head, the music trickled down the street, a fading
nighttime beat falling off the pace.

The Revolving Theme - (Abandoned Faith)

My emotions are frail, they silence my heart and suggest
eternal solitude. Amidst such amorphous surroundings
I wander aimlessly, searching for more agreeable forms.
The ruthless haters burning the pages slowing the
pace for the smiling faces; they hold their freedom
with allegiance though pale and worn.

We grow tired with the anticipation of brighter days,
assure ourselves that the genius mind will shelter
us from the storm as the parade of fallen lords unveil
their horns. The smiling faces drift backwards into
the glowing mist, as freedom falls the oath unsworn
the life unfit.

Credence

My perpetual state, my palace, my wisdom and sacred
knowledge, my sister of nature, my brotherhood. Dear
passion that swallows me. My constant sound and light
continually following me, I love thee with all my
heart and soul.

Farewell My Love

Cradle these vivid thoughts like fragile emotions,
so easy to go their own way and leave you falling
apart at the seams, chasing staggering dreams.

Silence all the motions, realize only the imminent
setting embedded permanently in your mind, an endless
river running hopeless, the water cold with ageless
time.

And she the queen your heart the mime, spreading wings
ten miles wide. To waste one more minute on eyes
so blind would hold me stagnant forever under the stars
unkind. Farewell my love, the days unwind.

Measurements

What have they found for me? My favorite piece of
broken chain. Lost in the cold sounds of my boundaries,
figure it out and chase away.

Sounds of silence swallow my thoughts; separate these
things for me, the meadows mist, curious surroundings
fade away. Gallant potion of a painted picture fall
with the rain.

Gleaming dusk time visions bring a swaying smile,
a change in the sky would make me try, but in shallow
waters floats a dirty queen, leaving poisoned flowers
for all to breathe.

In a palace of wisdom, it might lead me to a sacred
and passionate state of mind, sparkling light shivering

through the moments air. Might I find a gleaming
star to someday lead me there.

Where Fables Lye

Let us count the rings around heaven, the musing angels
of a crisp clear day, who cry with whirling warmth
and passing charm.

Let us pray for finer things, wondrous possessions,
mend the pages old and torn, brittle faces pale and
worn. By time and stages we change the pace and fill
the space where fables lye.

The Prince of Thorns, God of Scorn, flies the breeze
with black diamond eyes.

Lonely Eyes Have None To Read

Flicker beyond my shining hope, the nighttime is my
noonday scope. Far between my shadows reach, we carry
souls into the deep. The pale blue sea of cherished
queens, the firing squad of banished dreams, retracing
the days, changing the pace, flying the breeze. These
lonely eyes have none to read.

And I, as sure as you would see, stake no claim amidst
the breeze, I see as only I can see, as only you can
see, these lonely eyes have none to read.

A Moment in Time

Through my curtains I see the rain challenging the
sun. Soon the midnight clouds will swallow the sky,
conquer the tides that forever have tortured us.

The cruelty that sheds with the years, drained through
the channels of time, filtered thinly through perimeters
and spirals, faltered fears and chartered miles.

Let us pray for our year, which is any year under
the sun, amongst nature and beauty, each holding her
own.

This Valley I Roam

On a starlit road, spacious valleys of gold, a charitable
smile leads me on. A treetop vision, outlines untold,
pondering the tension that creepeth the soul.

Sparingly I thought, for a mind distraught, surely
a purpose is due. This valley lay soakin' not an echo
been broken, not since the Czar journeyed through.

Time has forsaken the darkened, brown the leaves,
changed the forecast to gray. Fogged by the memories,
the most typical tendencies, a clear blue river parting
way.

The daily array of the sun wakes me every morning,
draining me scarcely each day. Yet still this valley
I roam is without me alone, not a soul here ventured

since the Czar lost his throne.

Her Name Is Spring

Who sings more beautifully, more fantastic, with vibrance
unknown, uncommon. Who sings with such spiritual
ease, who buckles the air with gifted wings, flies
the night, reels out the scene, undaunted.

Her name is spring, short-lived queen of a forgotten
dream. She quivers with fashion and counts out the
days, styling her passions under the afternoon rays.

The burning fever is cured, the crystal river runs
pure under the revolving trees, into the shallow spring.
\

Village of the Broken Back

The portrait of a broken child hiding smiles behind
thew years of burning grief. Amid the flames his boyhood
fades, a blood-soaked page lying at his feet.

The streets out back shading gray to black, north
to south and back-to-back, removing sinners from the
garbage pack.

The sign reads, "welcome to the village, the village
of the broken back."

Angels in the White Room

Here I lie awake in the early morning hours, a dim
lit candle gauges the rhythm of the room. The shadows
dance across the ceiling like abandoned spirits blazing
through the funeral hall, searching for their tomb.

In the white room the baby sleeps peacefully in her
fragile crib. Her loving mother sleeps in the next
room, uneasy, waking instantly should sweet Alex shed
a tear.

Soon she'll fall amid some dreary dream, sweet Alexandria,
three fallen angels, three broken wings, guiding each
other into the rising sun, into the promise of a brand
new day.

Gazing through watchful eyes, I paint the scenery
as only I can see it. Gradually the morning light
peeks through my window, with eyes like a cat which
continually follow and eventually swallow the remainder
of a dream.

Out of the darkness I surrender my sight, the rays
of the sun burn much too bright. The shadows of the
evening fade into the day, Alexandria no longer weeping,
the tears all wiped away. Three angels, three wings
are mended, the memories keep the pace. In the white
room the baby's sleeping, three more fallen angels
begin without a trace.

Hollow Womb

The grating sound of earth-shaking ground, systems
of vibrations quivering mad. A sad, delicate situation.
Soon the visage leads way, striking these fancy shades
towards more clever days, further from fantasies had.

Through teeming vision, I have seen balanced vessels
fading green, clearly tracing the great cliffs with
crystalled gleam. Dancing with swaying spirits,
the siren of dreams, a common coherence for fallible
streams.

How clever we seem to be in this year of darkness.
The mute hears not what we see, only feels the burning
boundaries closing in on the earth, our mother, our
binding; courageous, demolished.

Climbing the Shadows

Bring me a velvet smile. Kiss me when I awake. Let
us chase the moon forever, swim a forgotten lake.

With wisdom growing thicker, the years now dimly flicker,
turning back at last, looking down with a ghastly
frown on what is now the past.

Should we ever pass, God shall shed the pain, lead
us down His path, save the final day.

Further from our dreams, those weak and feeble things
shaping optics in my mind. Lurking in the shadows
the prophets and poets gather to stand the test of
time.

A Play Called Shame

Rescued from those lonesome years, whence wander the
fears through a timeless river of tears, a rolling
potion stretching and tearing, the narrow river toiling
in vain, a phantom heart strumming the strings while
the mimes on the bank perform a play called shame.

Terrified of laughter, no trace of happiness, no song
for a smile, joy has departed, numbered her miles.
Now crying with vengeance, the mimes burn in their
rage, a reflection of innocence shading the river,
passing the fever, throughout the battered prisons
of shame.

Until My Dying Day

My poor soul, it takes the toll of many years gone
by. But still my eyes do shine with vibrance and
ambition, naturally, purely. The tears I cry continually
blinding me with rage and fury.

To swim the sea with open arms, to fly the thin sky
with balanced wings, with charm; to see her angel
eyes for the first time, to feel the love such beauty
brings.

To know these things, these days, will all soon die
with age and fade to memories, fall to floor from
page. To feel the flame, it burns my heart sullen
black, leaves me searching till my dying day just

to find my way back.

Death Trip

Believe the child floating the dream. Ponder his
sleepless emotions closing in on death. His free
spirit circles the sky; measures the towers until
he awakes the sacred hour for his final breath, grabs
hold of death and flies eternally across the universal
ocean he once called life.

The Spinning Wheel (Somewhere in Time)

Taken back way too far to find the channels through
this misty mind, drenched in black, the days unwind.

In youth I knew one who's days were rapid paced, moving
with agility, the quickness of fresh ambition, never
to let a moment waste.

The wheels churning forward shedding the years, the
boy is man with brand new fears, slowing the pace,
tasting the tears.

The Narrow Scope

These days seem cluttered with phobias. I challenge
the arena of doubt to summon a season as cordial as
the severed reasons I have found, bring justice to
the streets through powered freedom, thin crystal
clouds.

These tarnished rewards that case yesterday's dreams,
cruel fantasies stretch further down your polished
stream.

For Doom's Sake, The Ruffian Crawls

My fever is patient, standing still, honoring time.
A vision of gracious mountains, the morning I wake
and I climb.

My fortress in gold, standing bold, forever clear.
A dusty crown, unfaithfully worn, slowly treading
the years.

Daunting the curses, prolonging the verses, grasping
the day. Changing the course, a path full of pride,
invisible, forever unpaved.

The Seeds of Pride

The swollen sun beams down on me with a hint of sarcasm;
the morning bird spreads her wings when dawn awakes,
flies candidly from tree to tree, from limb to limb,
teasing all the boundaries, tracing the clouds so
thin.

Our fine lady of summer, so precious so free, she
opened her arms at the hour of three, when the sun
peeks low, nothing of shelter, no solemn breeze.

My desperate brothers follow closely catching only
the dust I leave. Through the shaky limbs we climb.
each will share his creed, his crime. Bearing his
own amicable cry. Soon, the silent bird with hollow
eyes shall plant her seed of ancient pride.

BOOK II

A River Unfolding

A River Unfolding

Or Time and Space,
Or shape of Earth divine and wondrous,
Or some fair shape I viewing, worship,
Or lustrous orb of sun or star by night,
Be ye my Gods.
– Walt Whitman –

A River Unfolding

Blessed is the beauty of this sacred weave. How neatly, how crisp we seemed to be as the dusk overlapped the trees which like an ancient maybe forgotten cradle so whole heartily embraced us.

We layed afloat upon the raving river, a constant rage beneath us. Challenging barriers within our path, over coming the waves of pain that tempt our passing through. Never did we relinquish such a burning understanding of what was in our grasp, as we in hers.

The Cold Booth

Waking slowly but terminally waking, here I greet this
splendid day ahead of me with open arms and empty eyes she
takes me.

Thin skies we fly spaciously, feverishly, patiently;
never will we cry, forever free falcon clawed we climb
sparingly.

And oft we've found this deathly air grows thicker, the
earthly flare dully flickers, the further we rise from
this hollow ground.

Battles bold, distant cold chills reeling out the shrills
of those martyred hills where the proud leaders lay with
hands turned clay, yet the eyes sustained to rule their
worlds.

And the mind still shames to leaving yesterday's pains
for the black-eyed bird to tear apart at bay, to disassemble
if need be may.

Silver Curtains

The night was pure, lovers quarreled behind draped windows.
Such passionate wakings for shallow dreamers; and I was
one so desperately caught between night and day, never to
find my way, left alone, stranded with God at thy side;
and here I swallow my fate.

In the mid-drift I see my destiny; such sour feed for
pearly gates. In this broken home these swollen bones
left to suffocate and bear this burning hate.

The Black Sound

Ride on, press hard, find the fortress kept behind the
sun; it shines ten million miles high in the sky reaching
the wizards in their den where the black cats sleep with
hens; where the sermon starts from scratch and the egg-
shell mind loses track, begins to crack, pulling the jack
as they cut the stack of time again and again.

A Song for Bo

Poor Bo lost in snowy mountains, searching for youthful
fountains, flowery graves are all the same and if you don't
mind please don't tell me, and God forbid you feel me or
feel like I do, is someone keeping score for you, those
blind eyes so phony free and few; and here lowly me
flickered dim with burning trees, their blood for mine,
their swollen burdened frozen eyes see death as death
sees heaven; sacred, true, definite, infinite, wisdom
unfed, imbedded.

Am I in Love With Thee

I am in love the kind heart said, tis the web of belonging
to one so dear, our love outlasting the years.

If thy love be sweet, I should bury thine eyes to the sea
as you and I breathe soft solemn breaths of joy, only feelings left to
sparing those moments for darker eyes.

If the love be of dull chimes, such muddy water spines,
I part uncalled, unheralded, just as I were before such
beauty crossed my weave. My eternal starving seed I bear
no more.

I am in love with thee; the signs I cannot deny, your
eyes beckon me to follow, save all the want and sorrow.

My love fears never tomorrow, never to die.

A Dancer and a Poet

Time to spill those guts, so far removed, these balancing
wings of time go untouched; those wanting ways and
perishing days falling to prey sublime and smiling enough
to comfort a shimmering breeze.

So out of town a city boy frowns bringing down the
perilous plot that is so often losing track of all that's
free.

The bending down to knees shaking brains that bleed,
and me and all my kings burn in hell for what we see.
The ever-calming scene of love and life, a dancer and a
poet moving forward in spite of things.

Tomorrow

Cry my precious love, cry for life's continual pain,
always atop of the finest flame and wiser than the next.

I bequeath thy shame, only to be proud once again. Only
to love your love once again.

I wish for only those sensuous sounds of desire. Those
lonesome sounds of passion so wholesomely drowned in
pitiful fires.

Every once in a blue moon I see your mother, dancing so
bold in golden tones of sorrow; still in the corner I
wish for tomorrow.

For Her Smile

This day is as fresh as your breath on my neck when the
early hours of daybreak fall from my hands with a gentle
calming sweaty. When early the morning flowers fling sweet
scents through this gentle breeze for you to breathe only;
I pardon thee and look with soft daring eyes, knowing with
a smile from the stars I shall keep you near my heart no
matter where the sun might rise.

Casually

Cold rush, soft touch, silent destined theaters of pain.
Aging rust, shattered trust, treading steady across the
plain.

Silent fingers, soft hairlike patterns scattered through
sand dune cabins holding off the shine.

My fellow brothers, let us make dust of this fallible
region, casting down this continuous hate and treason,
seeking shelter as we roam.

Now my master offers his gentle hand, leads the way towards
our fallen lord: the brain stacked piles bending miles to
kill his own, to catch the throne, to cut the cord and
be alone.

Little Man

Awake your virgin child, your mighty peaking smile, too
far drowned to fall asleep.

Keep my speeding heart close enough that we might keep
our eyes on the wall taking a chance on me.

The little man now heading back into the heat. All
these fattened sicken people peeping through the peep
hole shouting something sinister; lonesome the bird smile
flows too far underneath. The clown prince bringing
thunderous roars for the weak.

Such a priceless prison, such chambermaid trials adding
to the pile we cannot sink.

On the Ladder

I'm so sad, I'm so battered, you know those golden rhymes
of passion have shattered all of my dreams. So glad and
tattered with patient lies taking action on the wings.
And still I'm talking proofs all so uncouth taking this ever
aching heart high above and smooth.

Still, I know how these crosswinds blow, bringing out that
blue moon glow, while the song of home blows long and cold,
on down this whirlwind road we spiral.

The Cross

Here next to a starlit moon I channel visions through
vacant Victorian rooms, leaving much for all who come in
their glory. For those without a story, follow the con-
doctor's eyes, they see all the much more than some lonesome
god. No god of mine of course, the silent remorse and twenty
years gone bad, still the best ever me lord I've yet to
have.

Never should a blind man see what he can never have, for
what he sees is nothing unless we show him the clouds.
I've toured the fancies of many odd men, nothing hysterical
do I recall, I find them normal or nocturnal or whatever
that means. I cherish things not so frequent, legends
where never like you or me. Heroes are once in a blue
moon when you're living in a world where everyone looks the
same.

Where do all these silent creatures roam, those without
a home, swollen prisoners seeking only shelter from the
storm. God has left veins full of history all along the
tracks. The day will come when my god will set me free,
let me see just what I have become. This is the only
god I know, he glows in the love and beauty.

In the end the poem of life is lifted with wings, taking
flight the angels of legends fly with glee.

287, Wichita Falls from Heaven

Rolling 287, Wichita falls rolling from heaven, as we
speak we call the chosen few and all to be reborn.

Me and you crying with systemic frenzy, like the queerest
child listening. Speak quietly, know that you are not alone,
our banished queen has called us home. Let us live lushly
between these cradled winds of May, forgiving yesterday
and tomorrow.

I've cautioned much sorrow to know your morals were true.
Though customed I was I chose not to choose. Who's next
in line to cross this deathly wraith, who loves most to
hate when love is gone at last.

The Psalm of Space and Time

How to be in this hour of greed, how solemnly free going
blind in the breeze.

The prisoners have fled, turned their eyes to the sun,
turned their eyes to the dead.

Asking for wings, angels who sing the song, no earthly
rhyme, still the psalm of space and time.

Two Thousand Two

Lain on thy clover, green and yellow over, ship shape and sober
before the good god's eye.

Chasing the wings flying off the spring of life with ever glowing
dreams we found the heavens growing dimmer; and a little further
down we drown as the good god dies, we simmer.

Passing either side, the brainwashed hiding pride beneath inch deep
scars they've lost their stars the path now blind. Just how they've
blown where no one goes I will never know what love their lives
have
    found; how deathly lost they are in this hour of darkness, how
    grossly round.

Through this ghastly air we've wandered, such childish charm has
done

much harm when careless towers faltered. Though for many years the

wizards feared long before this deathly slumber, these countless rings

far distant rhymes and brandished themes pulling us under.

Catered we were those shattered battered earthly beings burning churning

children singing.

Cloud Pedals

Without warning those Byzantium clouds she once colored rosy today

have parted ways, their smothered hazy days forever aimlessly floating.

Still, I cried too, lonely, reckless, wanting; only to wipe all her

tears away, caress her grueling pain. Though in sorrow I lay haunted,

Buried in shame, helpless and hopeless as the silence kindles the flame

the blurry daydream scene comes to focus.

Tiger Train

We cast out the cold hard frowns of those ancient bygone blown days,

those flame throwing perishing ways so surely would bring us back to

nowhere again, no pearly gates.

I'll follow the river 'till the end; I do declare there is a better
life out there just waiting to be found. I wonder how easy it must
be so at odds with nature, while at the same time so in twine, drink-
ing the wine our fathers gave, and drunk all folding in on each other
like kindred brothers to the tiger train we stuck.

White Horse

Picture this she said with a hiss, a wet delicate kiss on thy lips, sweet touch of the swirling red rosebud bundled cheeks. You and I the newly crowned king and queen of the forgotten free, chasing staggering withering dreams; cry softly with me, dear fate has left a bitter torch to light our way, might we find the blind huddled in the

mines painting the white horse.

Passing Through

Mine and yours pure as fountains flowing, swaying with the ever-blowing crowd, standing then pacing and still forever growing.

Children seated peaking, bleeding, a thousand lines of fire. Taking a fresh hold, seeking drowning pity with the kingdom of desire.

This patterned chattered barroom, with its picnic panic stardom taking off the halos casting off the shadows, holding back tomorrow.

This poor bewildered system brushing off the friction, still the poet blue with sorrow echoes back the horror.

As You Are

Life, how sweet the vine, the ravine rolls and trickles down the bank,
another lonely year has passed, the stars take their rank, the dim
light
shines.

To lessen the sight, make the touch more serene more believable
pure
and clean. Taught not are the chosen few, how shall they learn to
feel for themselves through themselves solely, guided through echo-
less halls their failure growing, the veins of kings continually
flowing through.

While you and I sat still here waiting turning blue as the midday
sky so lazily passed us by, we can see it by the drop
another fumbled upon stumbled upon plot turning red and
left right here she said, not the wrong direction, trust

me our blood is pure together; our love is sacred forever. And who is it that loves me now and forever under these yearning stars? I love you only as you are, as we've accepted.

Blushed

Coursed I was in mystic woe when at first this road was
chosen! And oh, how my love had lost her glow, departed
our days for loftier brims, our soul tides forever frozen.

Lurking low, snake like prowl, the play unfurls with a
devilish frown! These Pisces pearls turn to darling dust
while the raving crowd drinks from dharma clouds reeking
rust.

This passioned scene, unclean, unseen, pure green with a
gleam. A parade of smiles, piles and piles of lovers
lust; the purple stained bus running our dreary days through
pristine streams, tarnished, blushed.

Faces Towards the Wind

Back and forth this system shaking sport piles death upon
dreams, the overall scheme of things forgotten, dug up and
rotten, we play the game and keep score.

Oh, poor me, bankrupt and blind without a penny, happy as
just about anybody could be.

My love applies the ease as my bitter soaked conscious
squeezes the ever-living breath out of laughter and despair,
hysterical mad moon visions going nowhere.

This Pig Latin drama circles through coated clouds tinted
dharma: the wings of angels fly above thy roof. When
Mr. Poe might speak in proofs, the cat rhyme children

sing out loud the awesome truth.

No twenty yard train catching up again, my friends have
chosen the long road, faces towards the wind; take this
oath of love and praise it 'till the end.

Such Are Clowns Like These

Lifting back this heavy sack of gold so long ago I stole
is now much of burden, always weighing down on me.

And all the time the king snake eye wanting to fry, asking
us why we look down with the greed, seeing all the choking
red clown faces thumping over wasted, sprouting out in
starving weeds.

And you know they ate it all for greed, plant their sad
soil seeds, choking off the free; such are clowns like
these.

Mugshot

Surely as the sun shall rise a common grace shall steal
your prize, our fallen lord who came to wait and save the
love we suffocate.

Something dear is in our eyes, we eventually search and
realized the fancies of our dreams, the challenge of our
rivals the sand beneath the seams.

A circus where the clowns looking so deathly red and swollen
round, cross the bar and shut their eyes just in time for
the rain. Still the drama unparted runs so duly worn,
dispirited, unguarded. The parade of gods passing through
your reading room, desperate souls, the soldiers bold and
proud, fighting the great storm of ruin.

This crisis was born so full of hate, hence the sun so

foully radiates, unbearable heat, how truly brittle my
hands and feet. The thousandth tide falls then rises,
with cat bright eyes the shadows raise above the water
as I breathe the misty air from beneath, as I taste the
pain the dull remains of defeat, the slow low drowning as
charity's darlings begin the crowning forever frowning as
I sink.

The Compound Freak

Lower me down to my knees you compound freak, give me a
prayer for the weak, a scar for my cheeks, so blood bent
bleak, far beneath your sick and withered smile.

Shower me with splendid scenes of anything obscene and
clever, around about the sunset lever, a buried temple
forever sheltered a little thicker in the pile.

And oh, how we try to be as sacred as a king when the path
uncut in and out forever weaves such a tangled trail for
you and me.

So, I say cover me in smothered black, relieve me of this
heavy stack so carefully packed between the endless cracks
of tortured miles. I alone shall guard the throne as the
compound freak onward spirals.

Low Tide

These scattered patterns of winter waving in and out,
the Texas sun shines low on the day, nighttime comes blow-
ing the warmth away from the south.

Shedding the shivering quivering leaves that autumn brings,
nothing left but the violent seas blowing at the mouth, a
violets spring leaving us everything; the hopelessly lost,
though eternally green, wading through the tears of dreams
and doubt.

Once Again

Once again I've lost the keys and here I am another stag-
nant breeze. See you and me falling down the ladder with
a pitter patter shatter, we gather marble dimes to pay the
king. One by one the people all pass with rust caked hair
through powdered grass, the parade of man is gone at last
and here we are alone, unsung, surpassed.

Crystal

Today she wore her purple hat as we sat alone in the rain.
We never spoke a word, never glanced a look, dull black eyes,
foggy window brain.

Type of day I'd say when foghorn visions wiser than me blur
the fancy people down the crystal stream, blind white
patterns, glowing serene dream. I love this day for me,
I see it so well, a beauty unforetold only impelled to
wavering heights.

An ode to my love, sweet angel in disguise; the hidden
meaning I have yet to find.

Superficial

Low and behold how the echoes have frozen in time much
like the brainwashed mind filtering comic rhymes through
spiral mills.

The cause was true, never confuse a confession so clear;
remember how dear mother was, how she was here then gone,
flown away with spades, flowery graves were never for her.

How easily said, the love light has fed on lifelines like
yours and mine. How readily we relinquish such simple
ways to pursue better days, when nature embraces us so
openly, so faithfully, so divine.

Soaked

Someone special endears me to hold strong, push away those
faltering ways, those terrible jeering days, pat down those
precious words, sing that sullen soaked song.

She's captured that smile long lost for a while, smothered
and covered in rosy toned piles. Still here we afford,
taking common remorse, knowing tomorrow is as blind as a
child.

In this heart of gold, I beg your eyes to shine my way,
share this glory that we now hold, tell the story never
told, hold the torch, never let it fade away.

A Tint of Gloom

Living, touching, seeing the sized-up fancy blushing royalty down
on
   their tender knees.

The silence and violence, shameful hearts so baboon battered
through
   the mystic breeze and cardboard forts. They see only as my own
eyes
   might see through the auburn breeze, through the pale moon light,
the
   silence of as brsand ne greed.

I Lose Myself

Take thy breath with yours, the wind of my soul shall fly with your
breeze and flow with uncommon union. And when challenged
with the vow
hence foretaken, my trust will create comfort. Comfort even upon
bare
mountainous rocks unto which dark desolate wreckage creates in-
evitable
fear. I for one will know that my faith is true. Not all was nothing.
Yet when overcome with loss I too felt anger. When ruined in
heartache
also was my soul outcast. And to my trail become dusty and covered
by
natures wrath. A long since forgotten path, at the present time very
long forgotten. Sometimes I wonder why so few have passed this
way.
Why only those few would walk the steps of this fortress. Never to

guide their eyes upon this tarnished frown.

Thin

Such thin little trees, waving pristine leaves that overly sway to
    see me now with whirling sighs and millionfold eyes. Yet I ponder
on
    what they could possibly see in this burning poet in me? Just what
is
    it they receive from this odd world we've so appropriately been
thrown
    into; here to find our cause, all the while perishing through.

    I wonder how these small wonders perceive me, as a cold and lonely
passer
    by, looking with cat curious eyes at the pure essence of nature.
Feeling
    as all great men have dreamt to feel and how I have dreamt to feel
with

them and them with me transfigured through the spirals of time, loosing

or brooding but never rebutting; this frozen oath is nature's mime.

Grandfather Clock

Brutal as beaten down frowns with plaster token crowns, a sinking ship
of clowns now buried at sea; a pale green scene painting flower
gleams and tainted Saturn rings up and down our universal stream.

This precious love for living, such sour sweet beginnings to a paint-ed
picture smile. Still on and on grinning, throwing down the sound
of the spinning wheel still ticking and rolling off the pile.

The Art of Misconception

I've gradually mastered she said as the veins in her head grew some
mad version of red; the art of misconception.

How truly worn out is my brain. I've contemplated desires driven
by
shrewd lame morning hours locked out in the rain. The vultures
smiled
without shame, they being a troop of black velvet dove in and tore
away
day after day leaving me scattered in pieces about my front yard,
gathering the remains left by my heart.

Of Less I've Known

Lost, how lost I have felt when methinks of those bitter bygone days
when a sudden impulse had dwelt, my sheer ambition more times
has spat
flames at dying ways.

Cross eyed, full of chivalrous pride, the stardust captain has flown
astray. Still all those captured have nothing left to say; no drama
holds true for the present. We know the past to be much more
intense,
the future unknown, uncommon, unpleasant, windblown fires
we've yet to
kill.

We pretend to know Mother Nature's profound ways, pretend to
know more
than we ever knew or will.

Gutters

Notice how bad so sickening sad this proof seems to be so uncouth, lying
   in wait, hoping to fall, warning us all never to hate, never crawl
   through the gutters.

Never to put a bounty on our soul for the price of timeless gold, how
   easily foretold, a dangling rope taking hold of us at last, chasing back
   the past, taking hold of today, changing those perishing ways to keep
   a foot on the hill to prove the martyrs were killed, so ultimately
   drilled, spilling their guts just in the nick of time.

Shadows and Cradles

Pressing, I believe I feel you pressing a tad bit hard on this fragile
window brain. This shattered scattered fallible thing. How faint
the
sound of a heart sinking down, lost in a cloud of confusion, the
auto-
matic illusion of love lost and found, an eventual intrusion.

And shine they will, those diamond clad hills plastered and tilled
over
and under the spinning wheel mind. Filthy gray shadows roaming
near
the gallows holding up the arrows towards the westward valleys
where
the velvet feathered vultures victimize the blind.

This desert covered region so full of hate and treason, smothered colored
    visions where tri-podded spotted dogs lashing and ripping
    away with four-inch twisted fangs, the ground giving way as the joker's
    thrown beneath,

Oath

Less we challenge the perimeters, certain boundaries which the human
  mind may obtain at any given point in any person's life, unless we see
  things through, show confidence in our beliefs, believe in our confidence,
  spell out the cause almighty and clear, pertaining to true blood, nature
  is our own as we are hers. Shall we fall like the rest, bleed with
  blue blood, soak in sweltering tears, drowning the tireless years while
  all the while the children look on with blood-stained eyes and smiling
  fears.

Twice Fold I've Been

Twice fold I have been here and there and out the door yet never before

    has such beauty fondled these deep-sea eyes, no disguise shall ye hold.

Though battered with love and drowned in hate, a soft-spoken broken heart

    toils with long winded days and patiently waits, slowly suffocates, then

    shouts aloud to up the stakes.

Hence the bard hears the call, loves you for the art of love, the essence

    of love above one and all, never to desert, bound by first dights and

cool driven midnights caressing her pearly white skin; the begin-
ning
of the end rolls on forever for you and I, these diamond tinted skies
never lie, they've opened the door to heaven for us and kiss our rosy
cheeks goodbye.

Redtop

Come here to me she said, figure out for me this shelled out vision in

red; bankrupt drought dry scenery, pure and black as death.

Ah my sweet, come to mother she plead, shadow these hunger burnt roses,

shake down the crawling human species spawned in frozen poses, sermons

so determined to spread out and die.

Still the sun shines too shallow, passing through the gallows, spacing

out the grind. This boiling stovetop region simmering out the season,

taking in the redtop shine.

Me

I breath in this soft pillowy air, I parade around daisies slim, relax the day away without a care.

I chase butterflies through the leaves of Autumn's sacred beginning and
fall free into her arms.

I space out dusty visions so that at a decent hour I may sort through what makes sense. I spend long lofty days counting the ways these blessed
memories bend this heart sewn fence.

Bottom Rail

Lost toys in the void, unclear, seldom heard; that timeless toiling
river rolling lavishly down. Circling, swirling, quenching that natural
thirst so wholesomely drowned.

And here in this sacred lot we weave the final plot. The battered
breast
buries the river engulfing us one by one, soul tides foaming, the
albatross
onward soaring; three shall live to tell the story of their sun.

How sad but brief the riddlers' beat rose true in the end. These
robbing
fiends roll death up the hill for charitable kill, wasting idle time
so the path may be filled.

Stolen Time

Do not look away from stolen time, its time is as good as the rest.
We should clear off the tables, shine up the wine glass stable,
   let the good man take the test. Let the poor man rest his weary eyes,
   in his dreams fantasize the moon and stars and sisters afar, go away
   your mind has strayed, pick up the broken pieces of an intolerable
heart.

   You bring back dirty memories she said. Feed my head with grand
opry
   wisdom, take these drippy feelings home with you instead. In turn
I
   give back thy stardom and perish slowly, the aging ways of dust lead
me
   onward, headstrong rolling the temptation shall rust.

Dear Father Grace

Washed through these bewildered tides I have often seen your eyes blinded
   with tears.

Secretly waiting shaming the hating, we pace and chase those time begotten
   fears.

My father showed so boldly how hard we tread our days with tarnished
   pride and healing faith.

Though dearly holding those days of waning now have disappeared with-
   out a trace.

Downed in the hours so brittly piled beneath the cracks of my
father's
    years. I'm crowned with courage still holding boldly up my end, to
be
      so drowned in father's dear tears of sin.

Who Will Love Thee

Put the pedals rosy side up down on the floor. Give me time to
search
   for those perennial rhymes long lost here after and forevermore.

And who is the one who bestows these sweet, delicious thoughts
like
   voluptuous crops filtered fervently through the water; birds and
seed
   to seal the roots, she sweats to soothe and shelter.

And just who will love thee every night and day. Holding strong
not
   to fly away too far away. Holding longer than forever and a day.

The Passer Bys

My lifelong friends, my cherished companions, we have lost sight of
those dreamy days, how far gone they are, how abandoned.

The years have tread over the path I've bled, how sorry they seem to
be,
    these faces changed wrinkled waved and dragging feet. These streets
all
    beat to a pulp, they quake as they sulk, abandoned like me, demol-
ished
    and free.

Morning rises and raises her flower; a new leaf has turned. No
crickets
    left chirping, the cool winds now whizzing, chasing the fire that
burns.

For now, the hour has turned sour, caressing the temple of time.
The
   scarce reflection, that sly slow detection of friends losing pace.
   The showers come falling still loosely recalling the face of a man
losing
   grace.

The Blackbird Pact

Blind, how blind can justice be? Such a burning fever such, swollen
greed. These streets all covered with blisters, our sisters and broth-
ers
floating through gutters while high and by the blackbird flies shed-
ding
her poisonous feathers.

Cursing the day, feeling better for now, crossing the crumblin' road,
on
my back the overload of many years weighs down.

So many questions never asked, the wisest flame is gone and passed.
All these names in a hat piling on the stack, who'll spill their guts
who will sign in blood the blackbird pact.

President's Day (1996)

The journey has been planned, pondering here today, such a presidential

    day, I'm flustered with beautiful thoughts. My mind today is testing

    the backdrop. Yesterday my dear comrades I tested you, I asked that you

    join the bard, let me feel your grand poem, move me as I have moved you.

    Then may we glide together scaling that golden river that aging with

    us each day misses you and me and the friends we've lost the same as we

    miss her.

Those mountains, those alps, those snow peaked beauties are wait-
ing

to be tested also. The day has come to cleanse the soul now more
than

ever. We can never lose sight of the love we feel for this dying world.
We shall stand brave at the top of that oracle that we may never lose
sight of what we know to be real, and pray for all knowing they hear,
knowing at that moment we have conquered the truth.

"The same thing, in all places,
all hearts that beat beneath the heavens'
day – each in its language – say: why not
I, in mine, as well?"

From Faust,
– Johan Wolfgang Von Goethe –

Acknowledgments

Special thanks to the following people for always believed in me; My brothers Wayne, Gerald and Alvin, Kemp Burris, Jonathan Web. Daniel King, Joel Olver, Noah Caveny, Chris and Andy Prda, Clay Copeland and the Copeland family, Angela McCrohan, Andy Golden, Dan Benjamin, Rene Diane Coley, My cousin Connei Barnett Connie Meredith Rene Martinez, Nathan Brown, Adam, Frankie and the 45"s,. To Deep Ellum and the way it used to be. When I could walk into any bar or coffee house and read my poems. So much love for Tony Anuci for taking a chance on me. Thank you Terri Jackson for believing in this book even more than me. Thank you Mom and Dad and my brother in heaven. Thank you most of all Madeline Teresa Pipkin for being the greatest daughter ever and for loving me as much as I love you!

About the Author

Anthony Ray Pipkin was born January 13the 1972 in Dallas, Texas.
Cut his teeth n Mesquite, Texas. Resides in Paris,Texas.

www.ingramcontent.com/pod-product-compliance
Lightning Source LLC
Chambersburg PA
CBHW060537130626
46553CB00002B/801